The Music of
LEO KOTTKE

Acoustic Musician™ Tape+TAB Series

The Music of
LEO KOTTKE

Transcriptions And Instruction By Mark Hanson

Published by:

Accent On Music
19363 Willamette Dr. #252
West Linn, OR 97068

Copyright © 1991 by Mark D. Hanson
All tunes copyright © Round Wound Sound or Overdrive Music (ASCAP) /Administered by Bug.
All Rights Reserved. Used By Permission.
First Printing 1991 10 9 8 7 6 5 4 3
Printed in the United States of America

Library of Congress Catalogue in Publication Data
Hanson, Mark D. 1951-
Leo Kottke, The Music Of--Acoustic Musician Tape+TAB Series
1. Guitar—Methods—Self-Instruction. I. Title.

ISBN 0-936799-08-0 Paperback and Audio Cassette.

Contents

Foreword

For years guitarists have waited for someone to teach them the intricacies of fingerstyle guitar virtuoso Leo Kottke's music. Finally someone has taken the time to do just that.

With the publication of *The Music Of Leo Kottke*, Mark Hanson has made the complexities of Kottke's seminal guitar playing accessible to not only the advanced player, but to the intermediate fingerpicker as well. And Mark explains the music and techniques in a manner that makes it easy to learn.

The printed music and tablature are clear and concise, and the teaching tape cuts right to the essence of the music. Leo's techniques and music structures are thoughtfully explained. Mark goes out of his way to assist the intermediate player with an occasional suggestion of an alternate approach that might better suit a player at that level. Yet there is no extraneous information here to clutter the process of your learning these tunes.

For anyone who is interested in playing Leo Kottke's music, I would highly recommend Mark's book-and-tape package, *The Music Of Leo Kottke*. Combined with some effort on your part, this package will have you well on the way to playing many of Leo's greatest instrumentals.

Have fun with this material. I did.

--Tom Wheeler
Author, *American Guitars*
Consulting Editor, *Guitar Player Magazine*

Introduction

Welcome to the *Acoustic Musician*™ Tape+TAB Series, featuring note-for-note transcriptions of some of the greatest guitar music available. We are proud to include the music of fingerstyle virtuoso Leo Kottke in our catalog.

The aim of the *Acoustic Musician*™ Tape+TAB Series is to make high-quality guitar music easily accessible to both intermediate and advanced fingerstyle guitarists. Instead of you struggling for hours to "lift" licks from a recording, we provide you with the music, tablature and fingerings for entire tunes. In addition, a comprehensive teaching cassette is included to make the learning process as easy as possible.

The note-for-note transcriptions in *The Music of Leo Kottke* have been painstakingly notated from Kottke's recordings. We have chosen to transcribe the commercially available versions rather than a private recording for the simple reason that those are the ones that most of you know and can readily hear.

The Book and Cassette

Both the standard notation and tablature are provided for most of the tunes in this book. We are justifiably proud of our innovative tablature. Not only does it notate the left-hand finger positions in beautifully typeset detail, it clearly denotes the rhythm as well.

One important advantage of our tablature is the right-hand information provided by the use of different type styles on the staff. All notes picked by the thumb are notated in bold type. All notes picked by the fingers or slurred (hammer-ons, pull-offs and slides) are notated in regular type. For a full explanation of our tablature, please see the Tablature Guide in the back of the book.

The only tunes not presented in standard notation in this book are the two 12-string instrumentals, "Busted Bicycle" and "Crow River Waltz." Each of these is played in an open tuning, a process which changes the fret positions of the pitches on retuned strings. Since few guitarists know the exact locations of the notes on the fingerboard in open tunings, we have eliminated the standard notation for these pieces.

A vital part of this package is the teaching cassette, designed to make the absorption of the written music as easy as possible. The 90-minute cassette for this book features each tune played at slow speed for ease in learning. For those unlucky students who have not yet heard Kottke's recordings of some of these tunes, a performance-speed excerpt follows the slow version to ensure proper tempo.

Measure-by-measure instruction follows the slow and performance-speed performances on the tape. In this section you receive valuable insights into Kottke's technique and thinking processes. This information was culled from extensive in-person interviews with Kottke for *Guitar Player* and *Frets* magazines, as well as from countless hours spent listening to and transcribing his music.

For each tune on the cassette, the guitar is tuned to Kottke's recording. For example, Kottke performs "Jesu, Joy of Man's Desiring" on *Leo Kottke—6- And 12-String Guitar* in open-G tuning tuned down an extra half-step to *Gb*. The guitar on the teaching cassette is also tuned to *Gb*, allowing the student to move directly from the teaching tape to the actual recording without retuning the guitar.

We have gone to great lengths to ensure the accuracy and thoroughness of our transcriptions. Short of having Leo at your house, this combination of book and teaching cassette we feel provides the optimum in teaching programs. We have a number of other Kottke transcriptions available in our *Acoustic Musician*™ Tape+TAB Series, and are expanding with other artists, so please let us hear from you!

--Mark Hanson

The Artist

In addition to being a great artist, fingerstyle guitar virtuoso Leo Kottke is a true American original. From his teenage years he wanted to develop a new voice on the guitar, one unencumbered by the patterned picking evident in so much American folk music of the '50s and '60s. He accomplished his goal with a vengeance.

Taking the guitar world by storm with his 1969 LP *6- And 12-String Guitar*, Kottke redefined the role of the fingerpicked 12-string guitar. His overpowering sound and speed, coupled with an ever-growing compositional ingenuity, launched him on a continuing course through nearly two dozen LPs and several major record labels.

His solo concert tours continue to cover the world, even as he branches off into the world of video--*Home & Away* was a PBS hit in 1989--and orchestral arranging. And his self-effacing Mid-western manner helps endear him to his audiences and fans. He is an artist who thoroughly enjoys his art--and one who makes sure that his audiences enjoy it as well.

Leo's Composing

"I play all the time and I stumble onto things," says Kottke in ascribing his considerable compositional talents to simple trial and error.

"My composing is either instinctual or stupid. I don't write at all like (fellow fingerstyle guitar artist) Michael Hedges. He takes motifs and expands them, as a trained composer does. I'm not much good at that type of composing because I don't have the training."

The fact that Kottke has no formal musical training is a source of amazement to many, considering the wealth and breadth of music he has written. The structures of his tunes are invariably perfect, with the correct decisions made at each strategic juncture. His melodies mostly are simple and easy to hum, yet distinctive. And his harmonies have always stretched the ears of folk music aficionados.

Kottke occasionally ventures near the fringes of the avant-garde with his tunes, but his musical roots lie squarely in the European tradition. "My intuition for musical form and melodies comes largely from my trombone training as a kid," says Kottke. "I was exposed to classical music, and those tunes and that kind of structure really sunk in."

For Kottke, the process of composing a new piece of music is as important as the finished product. "I compose new tunes on the guitar as much for the fun of finding a piece as for having a finished piece," says Kottke. "I enjoy the search the most."

We, as his fans and appreciators, should be happy that Leo continues to enjoy the search for new music as much as he does. And, if he can write tunes as artful as "Times Twelve," "William Powell," and "Theme From 'The Rick And Bob Report'" (all from his 1989 album *My Father's Face*) by relying on instincts, we can only hope that he avoids studying music!

We hope you enjoy the process of learning these tunes as much as Leo enjoyed writing them and we enjoyed sharing them with you. Have fun!

Kottke's Technique

As prodigious as Leo Kottke's picking and fretting techniques have been since the late '60s, he has always relied on good tone as the foundation of his playing. Whether it be the 12-string pyrotechnics of "Busted Bicycle," or the delicate lyricism of "Echoeing Gilewitz" (*A Shout Toward Noon*), Leo's sound is crucial to him.

Right-Hand

Since the early '80s, when Kottke stopped using fingerpicks, he has held his right hand in a position similar to the high-arch position of classical guitarists. But there is one substantial difference between his position and that of most classical players: Kottke's right wrist is straighter.

A straighter wrist brings the side of his right thumb much closer to the strings, almost to the point of being parallel. This position allows him to damp bass strings quite easily with the side of his thumb. He does this to great effect on many of his tunes, preferring the damped sound to the constant drone of sustaining bass strings.

Kottke's right thumb also extends well beyond the index finger of his picking hand. This ensures that the thumb and index finger won't collide when picking adjacent strings.

He picks with a combination of flesh and fingernails, brushing the skin of his fingertip across the string and releasing it with the fingernail. Kottke likens this picking procedure to bowing a string, like a violin. It produces a much richer tone than if the fingernail alone contacts the string. To make sure that he picks the strings largely with the flesh rather than the fingernail, Kottke keeps his fingernails relatively short.

Also, Leo is comfortable picking any of the strings on his guitar with any finger. He generally assigns the thumb to the bass strings, and the index, middle and ring fingers to three treble strings (third, second and first, respectively, for instance). But this can change in a moment. Very often he will pick as low as the fifth string in the bass with his index finger. You'll find this in "Busted Bicycle," among other places. And when picking scale-type passages, as in his 12-string instrumental "Times Twelve," he will alternate picking his thumb with his index or middle finger.

Left-Hand

Leo's left-hand techniques are many and varied, of course. But a number of positions must be understood to make an attempt at imitating his playing.

First, Leo often uses his left thumb to fret the bass string. This technique is particularly apparent in "Theme From 'The Rick And Bob Report.'" If you can't fret the bass string with your thumb (your thumb is too short, the guitar neck is too wide, or your classical teacher won't let you!), you will have difficulty playing the *F*-chord passages as Leo plays them.

Secondly, Leo often barres with his index finger. A common fingering for him is a four-string barre with the index finger, with the middle and ring fingers fretting the second and fourth strings one and two frets in front of the barre, respectively (An *Aminor 7th* fingering in front of the barre).

Barre chords consist of squeezing the neck and the strings between your *thumb* and your barring finger. If you have trouble barring, here is a suggestion: Make sure your left thumb is placed about halfway down the back of the guitar neck, directly behind the barring finger. If your thumb is straight (as it should be), this will force your left wrist down toward the floor. If you aren't accustomed to barre chords, you'll need to learn them to play many of Leo's tunes. Good luck!

Busted Bicycle

"Busted Bicycle" is one of several powerhouse 12-string pieces Leo Kottke used to take the folk music scene by storm in the late '60s. Along with similarly blazing pieces like "Watermelon," "Vaseline Machine Gun" and "Coolidge Rising," from his classic 1969 recording *6- And 12-String Guitar* (the "Armadillo" record), "Busted Bicycle" helped Kottke to solidify his standing as one of the greatest 12-string players in history.

Kottke tuned his 12-string guitar in open-C tuning, C G C G C E (lowest pitch to highest) for "Busted Bicycle" on *6- And 12-String Guitar*. But he lowered it another 1-1/2 steps to *A E A E A C#* (lowest pitch to highest). That low pitch (the lowest *A* is two octaves and a third below middle-C) helped produce the throaty roar so characteristic of Kottke's guitar tone on his early recordings.

The tune is in the alternating-bass style, although Leo often picks the same bass string with his thumb on consecutive beats—measures 2-11, for example. Pay close attention to the staccato and left-hand damping techniques in measures 14-19. They are very important for the rhythmic feel.

On the accompanying cassette, the guitar is tuned to match Leo's recording, so that you may move easily from the teaching tape to Leo's playing. Some fine tuning of the speed on your playback machine may be required to make the pitch of the teaching tape correspond exactly to Leo's recording. Adequate time is provided on the tape for you to match the pitches of the open strings.

Once you have learned "Busted Bicycle" using the tape, you may prefer not to tune down all the way to Leo's pitch. In that case, consider using open-C tuning: *C G C G C E*. This is the tuning listed at the beginning of the tablature for "Busted Bicycle."

For information about all of Leo Kottke's solo recordings, please see the discography in the back of the book.

"Busted Bicycle"

Transcribed From 6- & 12-String Guitar

By Leo Kottke

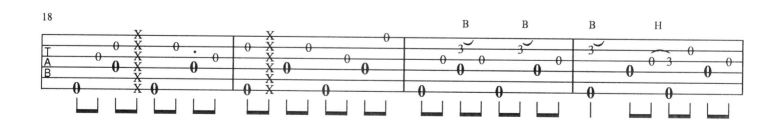

"Busted Bicycle"

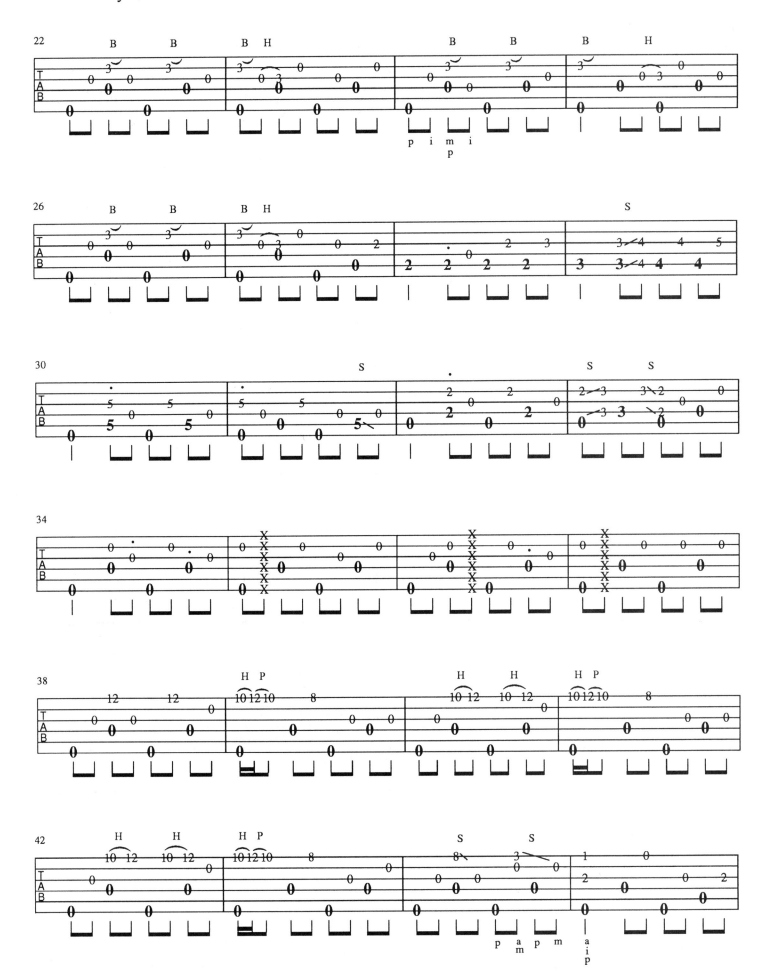

"Busted Bicycle"

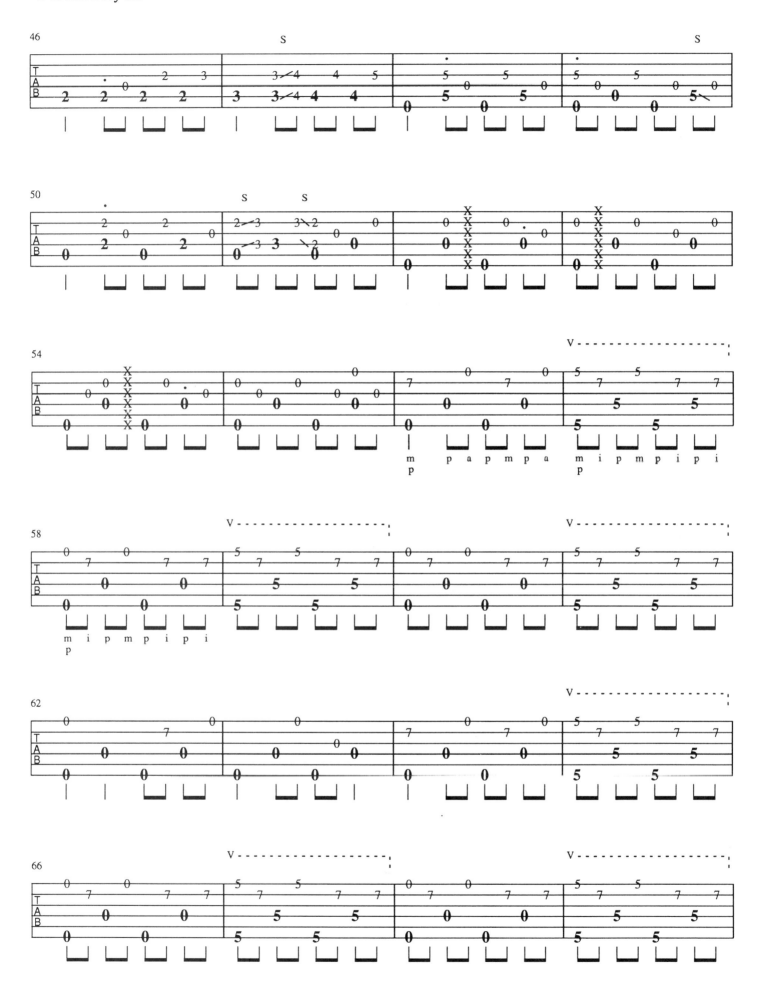

"Busted Bicycle"

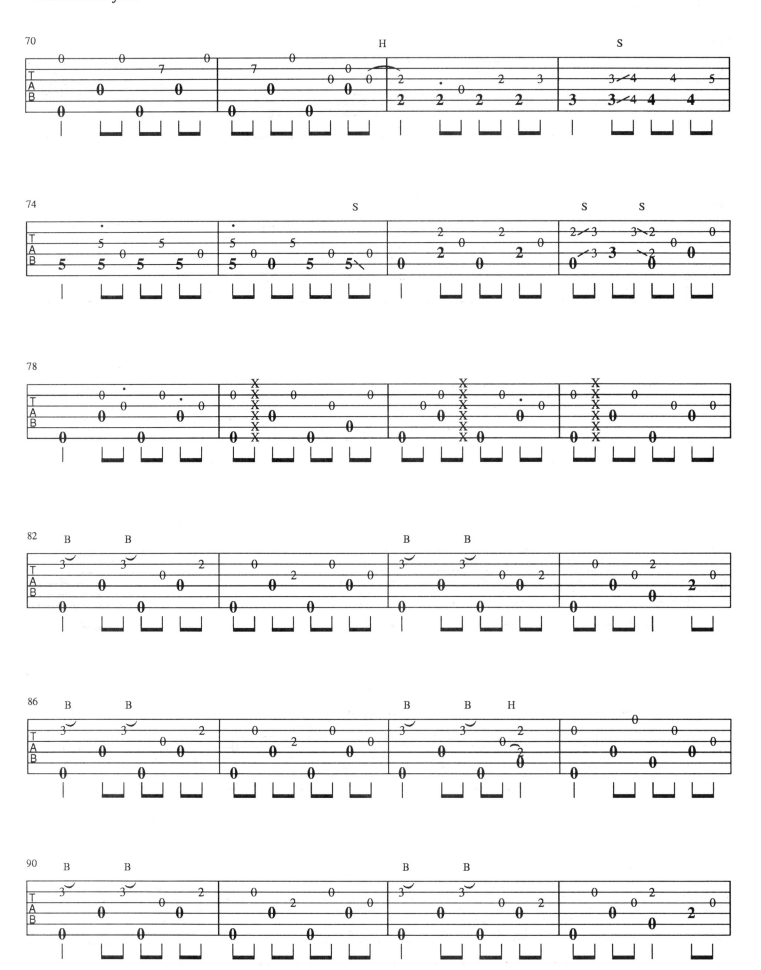

"Busted Bicycle"

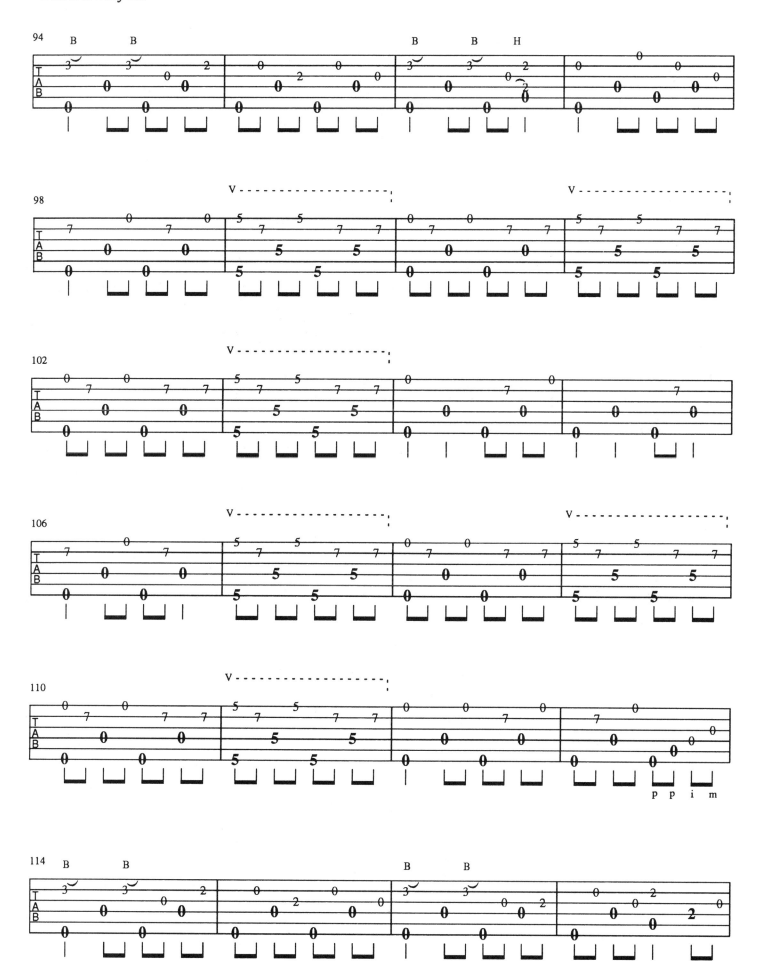

17

"Busted Bicycle"

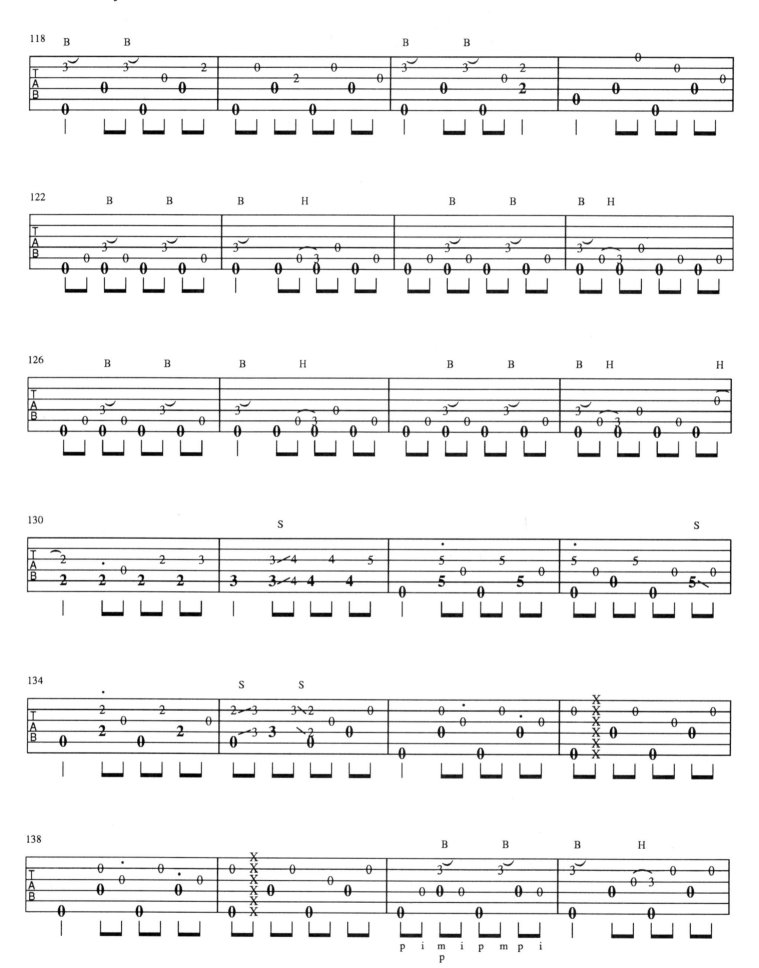

"Busted Bicycle"

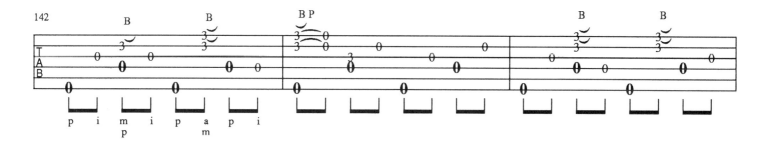

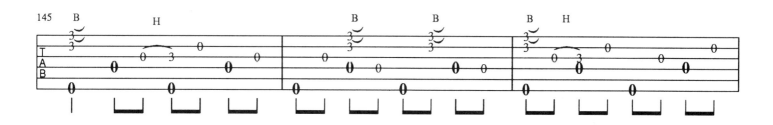

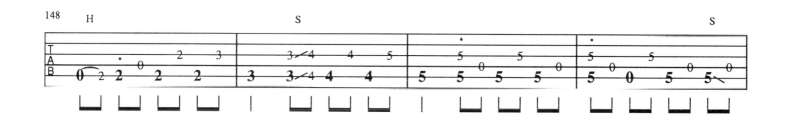

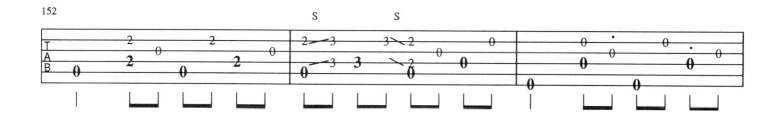

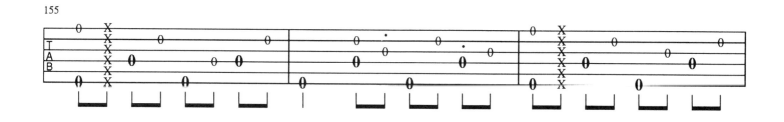

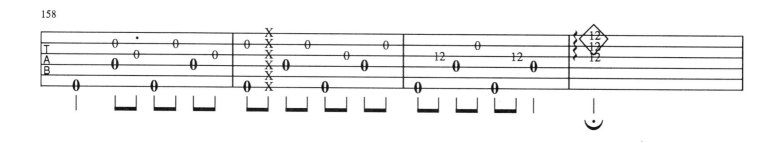

Jesu, Joy Of Man's Desiring

"The engineer called this the ancient joy of man's desire. (Bach had twenty children because his organ didn't have any stops.)" So says Leo Kottke of his arrangement of this J.S. Bach classic in the liner notes to his LP *6- And 12-String Guitar*.

Most people know "Jesu" as an organ piece, having heard it innumerable times in church settings. But Kottke, with his arrangement in open-G tuning, shows how beautifully it can be set on guitar in an open tuning.

Interestingly enough, the original piece was written for neither of these instruments, but was a cantata for orchestra and four-part chorus. The eighth-note melody and its accompaniment that begin the piece (measures 1-16) were played by the orchestra. The chorus (soprano, alto, tenor and bass) sang the German words to the slow moving melody that begins here in measure 17.

Leo left out a section of the original in his arrangement. After the second choral section, Bach composed a middle section that Leo chose not to include in his arrangement. This section modulates through a number of different keys, something that can be difficult for a guitarist using an open tuning.

Playing Suggestions

If you have limited experience playing running eighth-note melodies like the one in "Jesu," practice the upper and lower parts separately. Play only the melody, without the bass notes, paying attention to the fingering in the left hand.

Once that is under control, work on alternating the fingers of the right hand while you play the melody. Follow the suggestions offered on the cassette tape. Then you'll be ready to add the bass notes.

Make the melody as smooth as possible. This is accomplished by sustaining each melody note right up to the moment you pick the next one. Make sure your left-hand fingers do not let go of your melody notes too soon. If you do, "Jesu" won't be as smooth sounding as it might be.

"Jesu, Joy Of Man's Desiring"

By J.S. Bach
Arrangement by Leo Kottke

Transcribed From 6- & 12-String Guitar

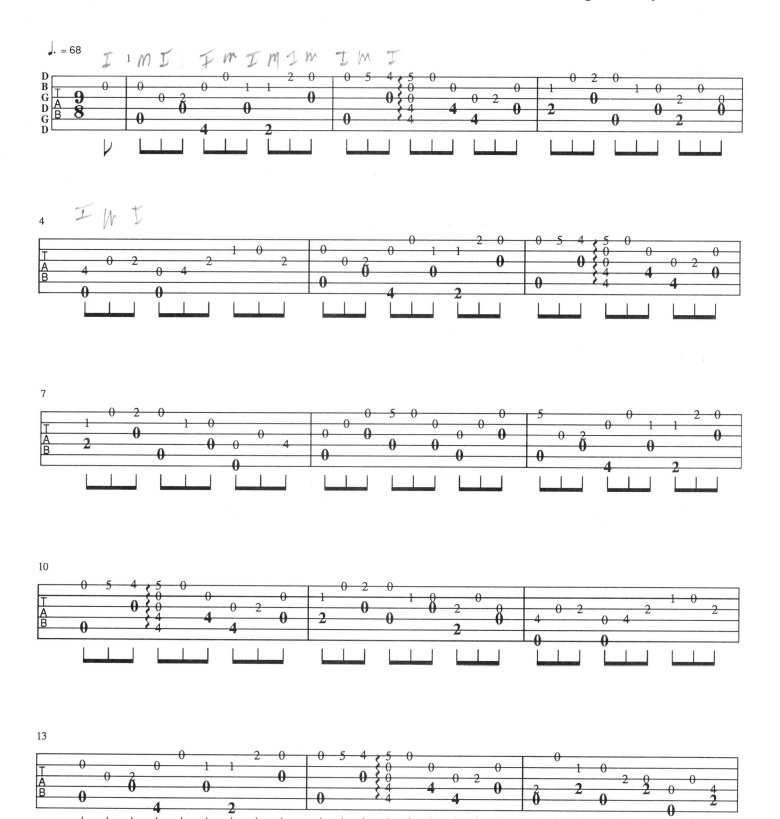

"Jesu, Joy Of Man's Desiring"

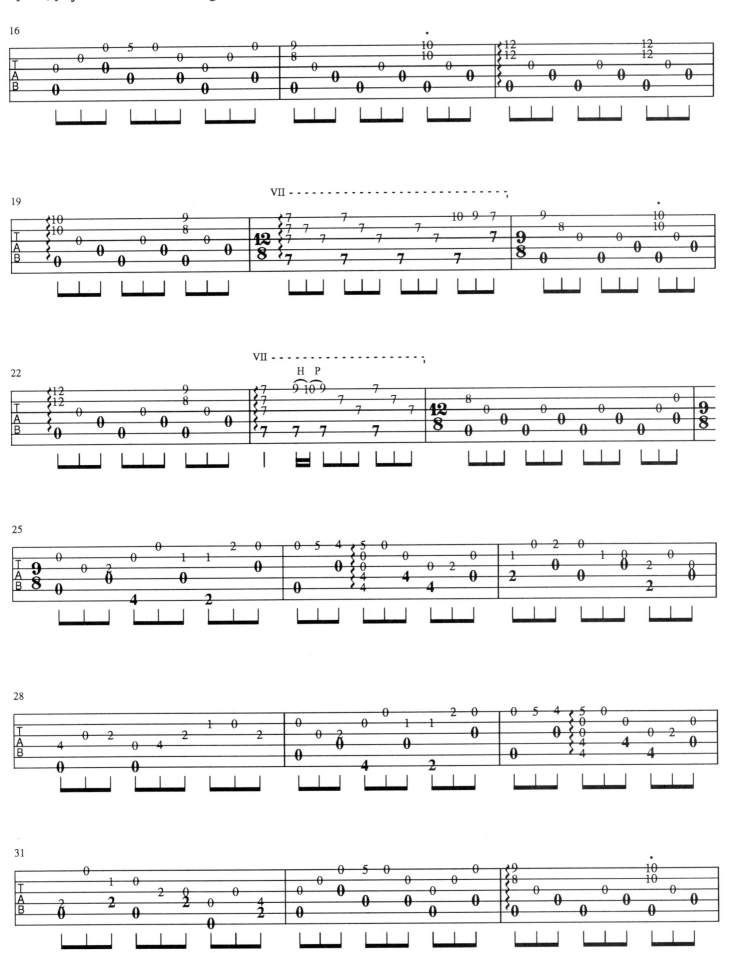

"Jesu, Joy Of Man's Desiring"

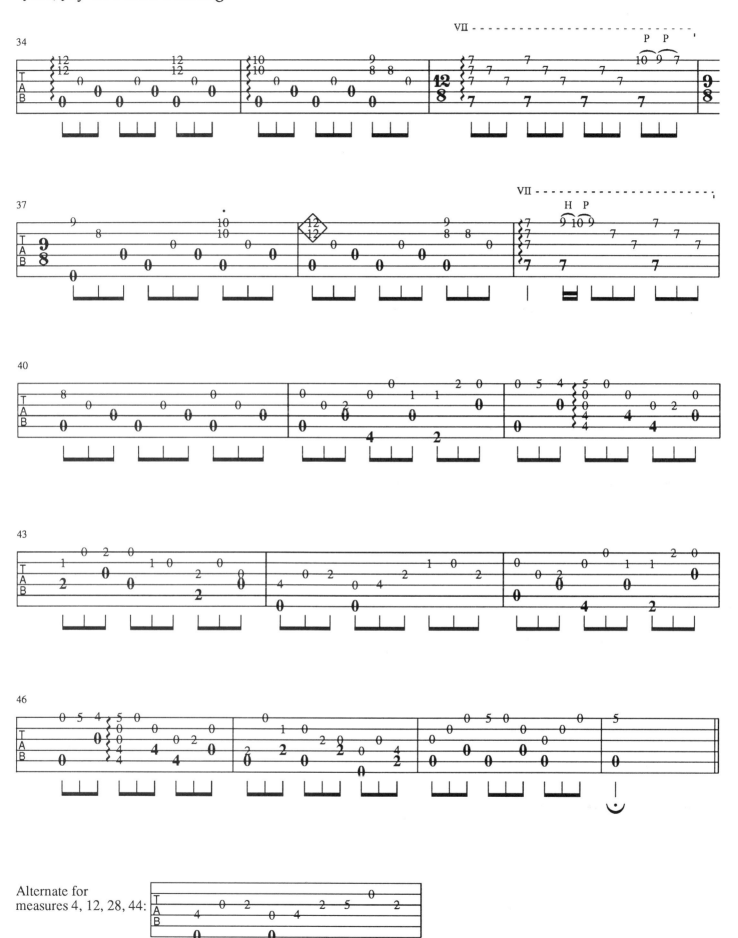

"Jesu, Joy Of Man's Desiring"

By J.S. Bach
Arrangement by Leo Kottke

Transcribed From *6- & 12-String Guitar*

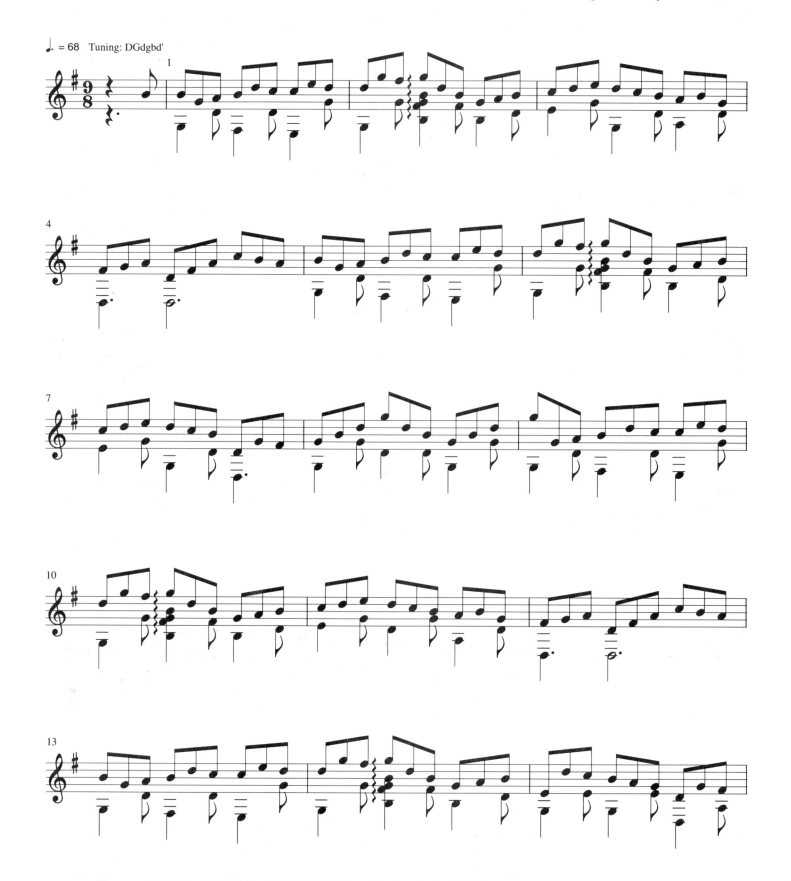

"Jesu, Joy Of Man's Desiring"

"Jesu, Joy Of Man's Desiring"

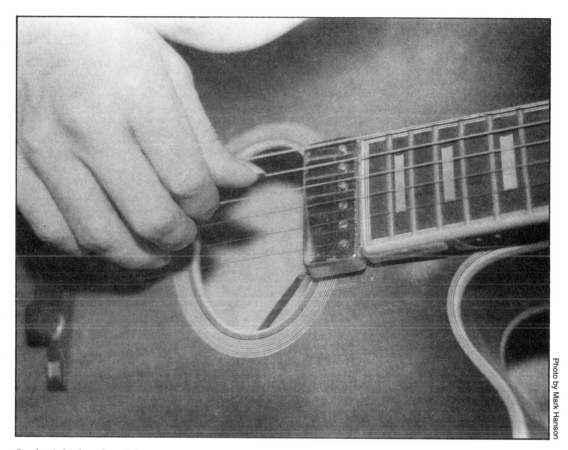

Leo's right-hand position.

Crow River Waltz

Because of the way Leo designed the melody of "Crow River Waltz," it sounds much better on a 12-string than a 6-string. Follow the suggested right-hand picking closely: In most measures the thumb must pick the third-string note on the third beat to ensure a strong high-octave note.

The tuning is open-G lowered two whole-steps to *Bb Eb Bb Eb G Bb* (bass to treble). Once again, after you have learned the piece you may prefer not to tune all the way down to Leo's pitch. In that case, use open-G tuning: *D G D G B D* (bass to treble). That is the tuning listed at the beginning of the tablature.

"Crow River Waltz"

Transcribed From *6- & 12-String Guitar*

By Leo Kottke

"Crow River Waltz"

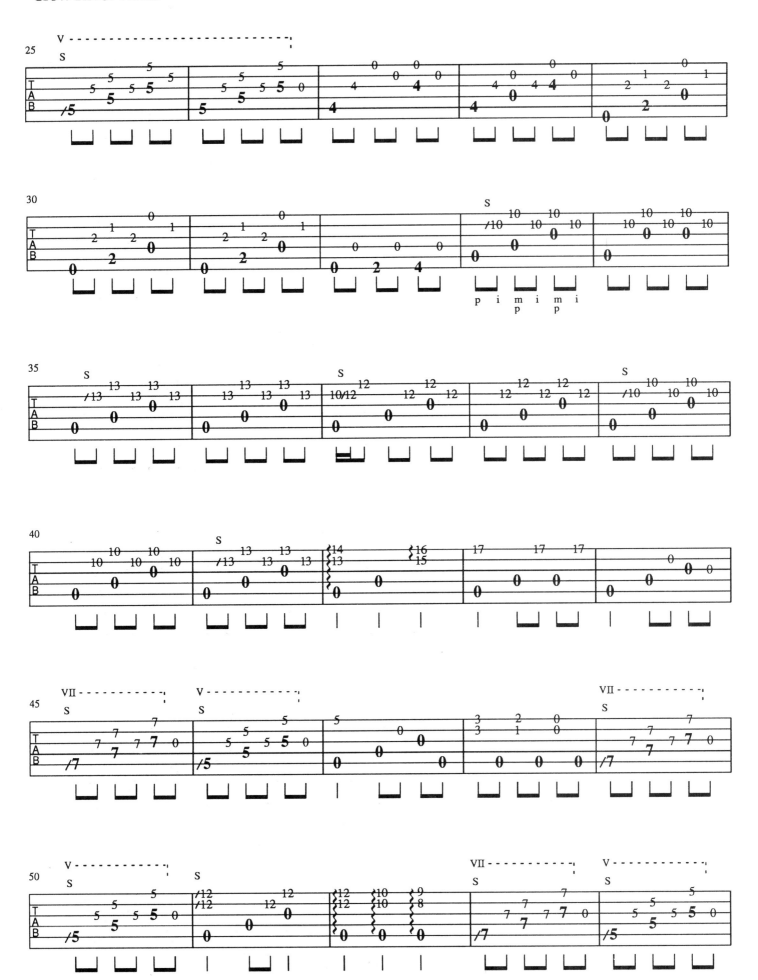

"Crow River Waltz"

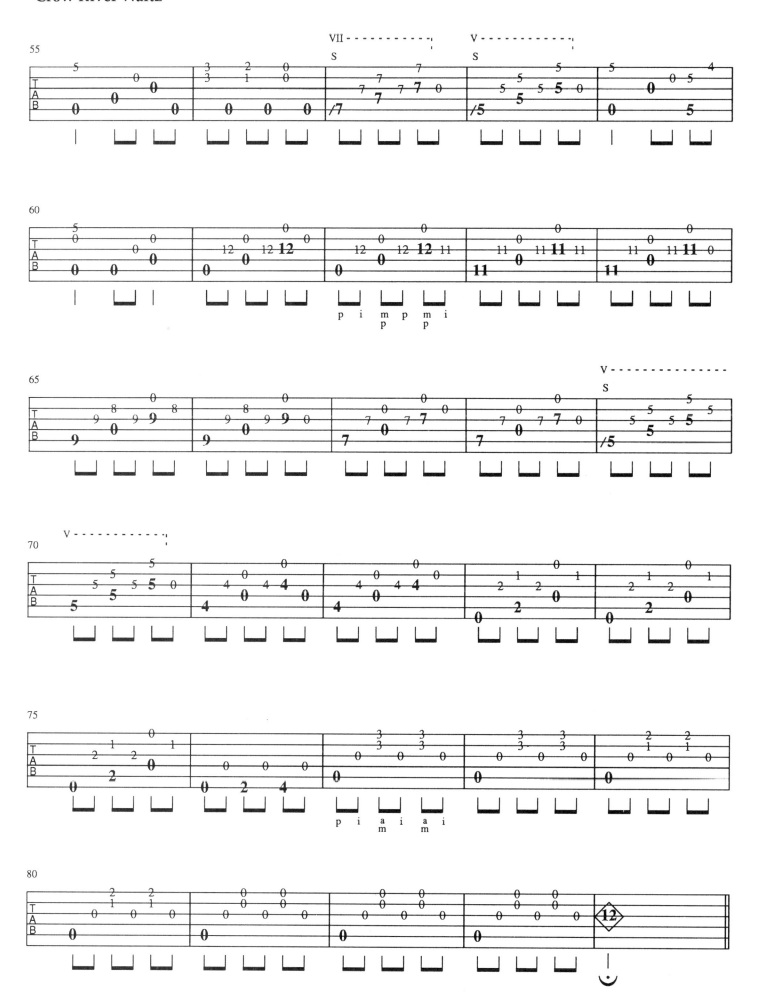

Theme From "The Rick And Bob Report"

"The Theme From 'The Rick And Bob Report'" is a wonderfully lighthearted tune from Kottke's 1989 album *My Father's Face*. Leo plays it in the key of C, but with a capo placed at the 5th fret. The music actually sounds in the key of F.

This tune is fairly repetitious, but never gets boring because of the way Leo has structured the piece. The opening 16-bar phrase is repeated many times throughout the tune, but whenever it approaches redundancy Leo throws us a curve. For instance, in measure 33 he very easily could have launched into the main 16-bar phrase again, for the third time in a row. But instead he gives us a "deceptive cadence" to *Aminor*. (Our ears are expecting a C-chord, but he gives us its relative minor instead.)

But the *Aminor* doesn't lead to an entirely new section, as we might expect. He simply places measures 6-8 of the opening phrase directly after the *Aminor*. But in this position, following the *Aminor*, those three measures provide a new and refreshing feel to the music.

After repeating those four bars in measures 37-40, Leo picks up the main theme again in measure 41. After the little *Aminor* excursion our ears are ready for the main theme, and it once again sounds fresh.

Leo repeats the main theme and *Aminor* sections through measure 64, where he introduces a "bridge," a new section of music using *Eminor* and F-chords. When he once again returns to the main theme in measure 89, it is set up beautifully.

"Theme From 'The Rick And Bob Report'" is an example of a master composer at work. It's a simple tune, but captivating, and a lot of fun to play.

Playing Suggestions

Make sure that the C/G-chords in this tune are fingered with *four* fingers. The ring finger of the left hand frets the sixth string, while the little finger frets the fifth string. When you move to the subsequent F-chord, move your left-hand ring and little fingers to the fifth and fourth strings, respectively.

In measures 7-8, try to bring out the scalar melody that Kottke is playing on the fourth and fifth strings. Do that by de-emphasizing the open second and third strings when you pick them.

In measures 13-16, sustain the first note of the G7/B-chord (an F-note, 3rd fret of the fourth string) until you pick the fourth-beat E-*note* (2nd fret of the fourth string). Sustaining that F-note makes the chord on the third beat of the measure a G7 sound.

"Theme From 'The Rick And Bob Report'"

Transcribed From *My Father's Face*

By Leo Kottke

33

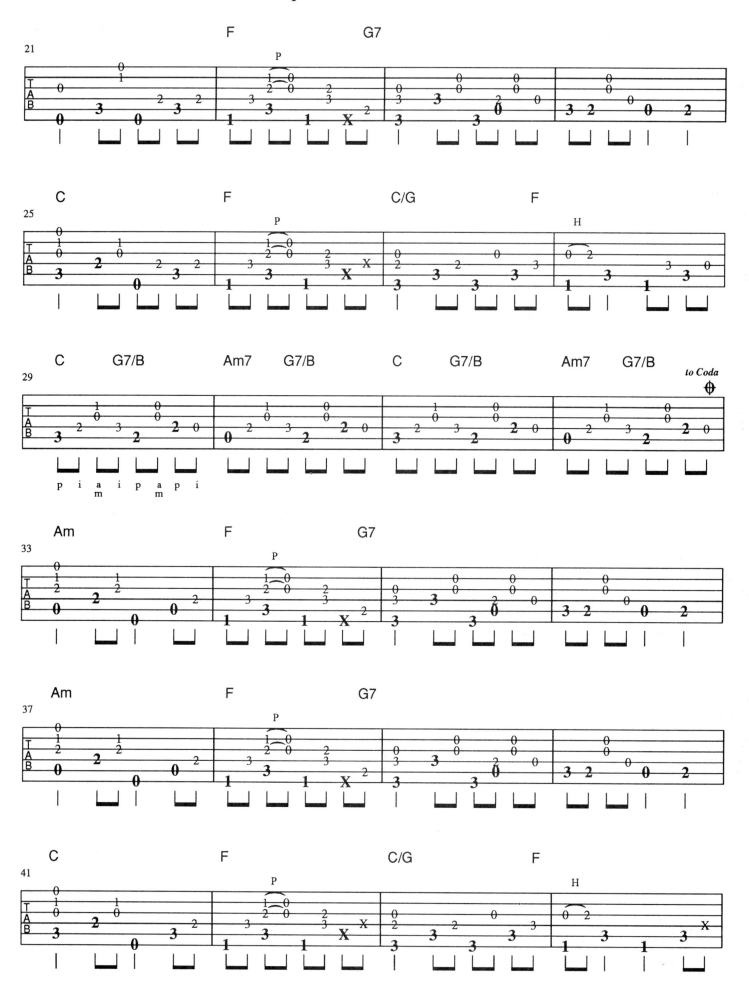

"Theme From 'The Rick And Bob Report'"

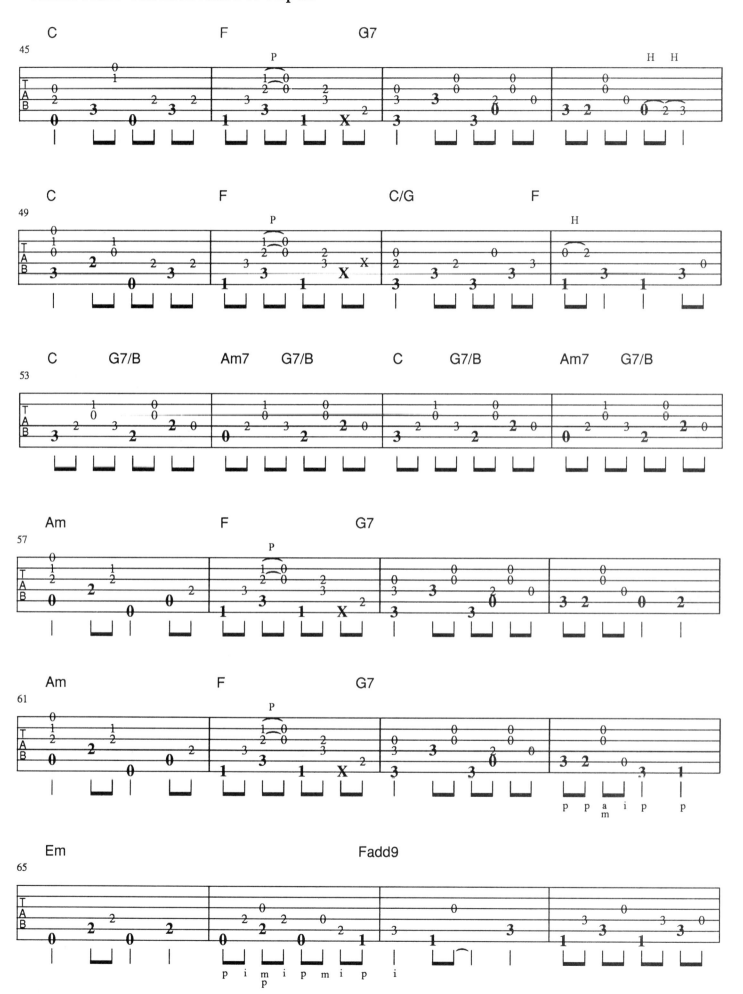

"Theme From 'The Rick And Bob Report'"

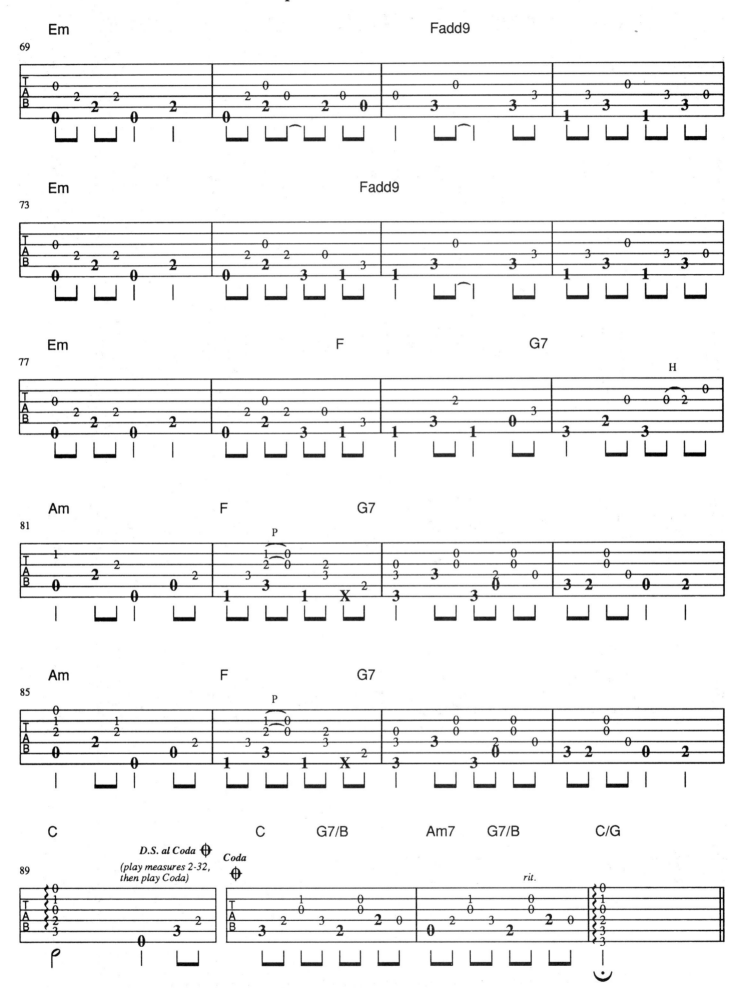

"Theme From 'The Rick And Bob Report'"

Transcribed From *My Father's Face*

By Leo Kottke

"Theme From 'The Rick And Bob Report'"

"Theme From 'The Rick And Bob Report'"

"Theme From 'The Rick And Bob Report'"

Photo by Mark Hanson

The Artist

Little Beaver

"Little Beaver" from Leo's 1986 album *A Shout Toward Noon*, is another masterpiece of composition. It is very simple and repetitious, but never boring. It's also fast and challenging to play, despite its musical simplicity.

The main melody (measures 1-4) is repeated many times throughout the piece. Leo avoids boring us, however, by altering the octave of the harmonization --measures 9-16 add the fifth and sixth strings in the bass. And also by playing the melody in a lower octave--measures 16-24.

Leo tuned his guitar in drop-*D* tuning, *D A D G B E* (lowest pitch to highest). At the time of this recording he was using primarily a Hoffman 6-string guitar, which he said "likes to be tuned down one-half step." So the recording is one-half step lower: *Db Ab Db Gb Bb Eb*.

Playing Suggestions

Leo's right thumb is very busy in this piece. It does a lot of muting of the bass strings in addition to its picking. For sake of ease, consider damping the four treble strings in measure 1 by placing your right-hand fingers on the strings. Then they are ready to pick the last three eighth notes of the measure.

Finger most of the *D*-chords in this piece with an index-finger barre over the four treble strings. Kottke uses this 4/6 barre-chord fingering in many of his pieces, including one of his most popular tunes "Mona Ray," and his 12-string opener on *My Father's Face*, "Times Twelve."

Work slowly through this piece. Once you have mastered the picking and muting techniques, then speed it up. Have fun!

"Little Beaver"

Transcribed From *A Shout Toward Noon*

By Leo Kottke

"Little Beaver"

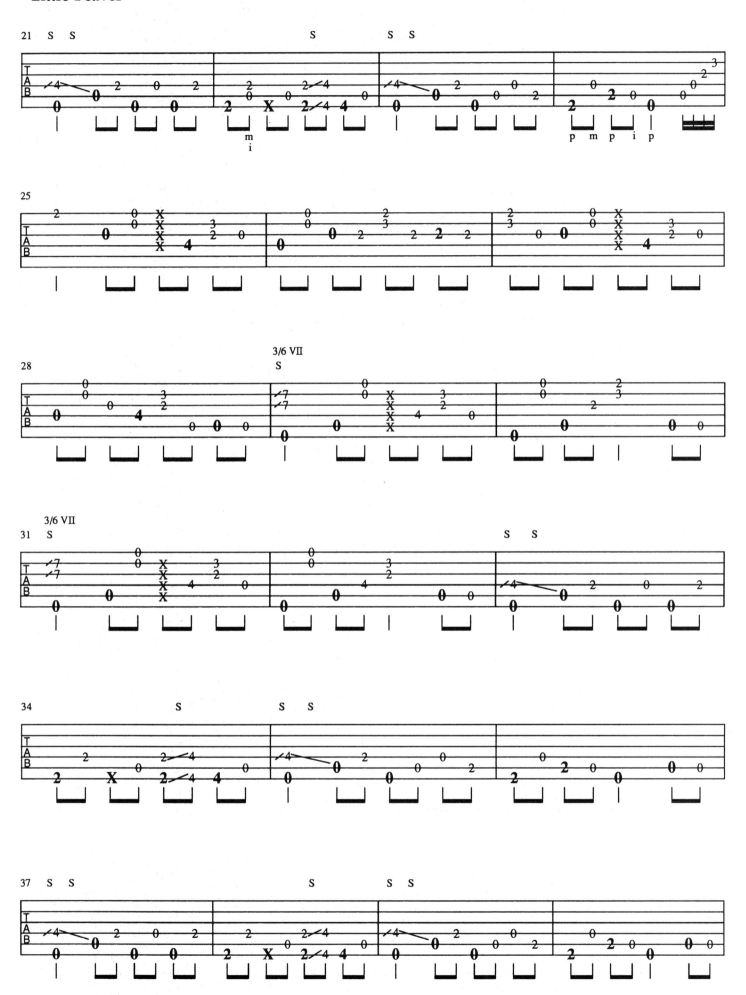

"Little Beaver"

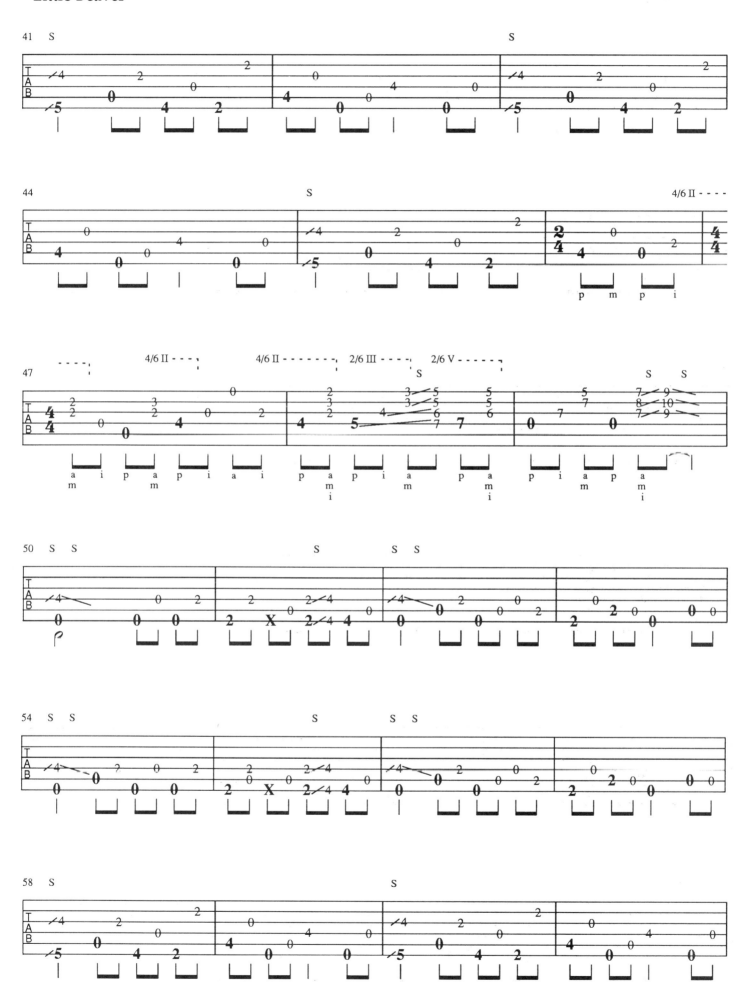

"Little Beaver"

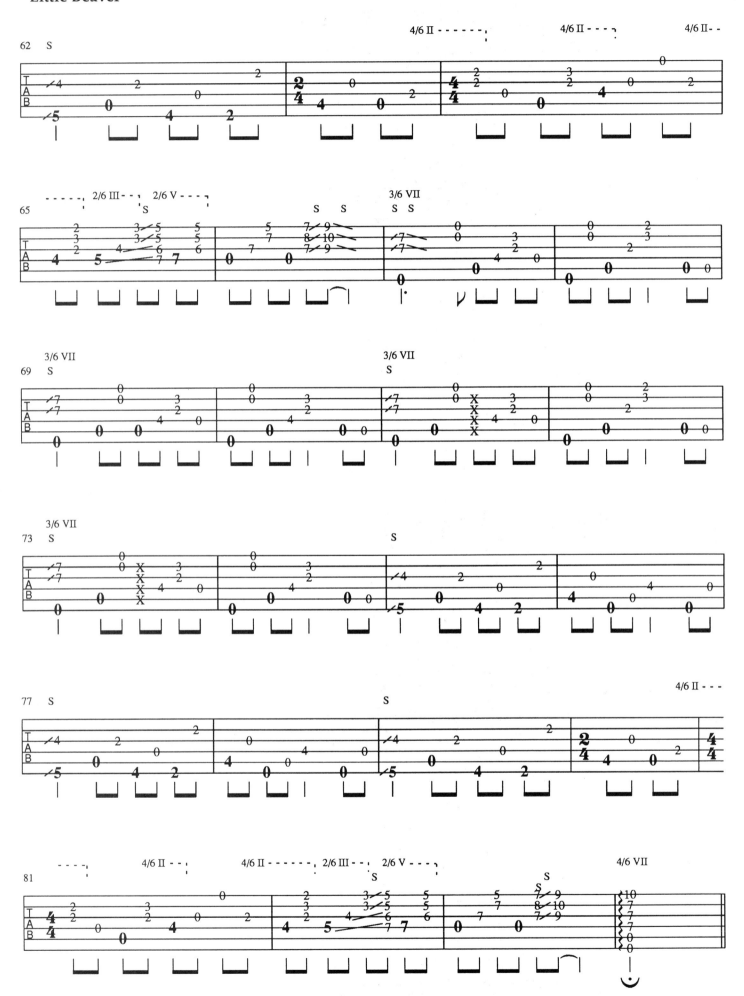

"Little Beaver"

Transcribed From *A Shout Toward Noon*

By Leo Kottke

"Little Beaver"

"Little Beaver"

"Little Beaver"

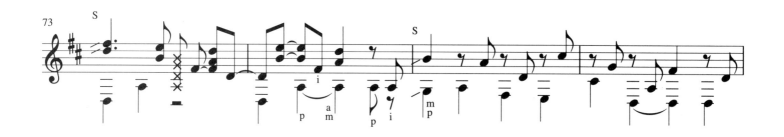

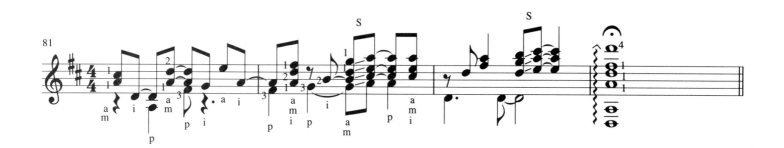

Leo Kottke Discography

1968 *12-String Blues* (Out of print)

1969 *6- & 12-String Guitar* (Available On Rhino 71612)

1970 *Circle 'Round The Sun* (Symposium 2001)

1971 *Mudlark* (Capitol 682)

1972 *Greenhouse* (Capitol 11000)

1973 *My Feet Are Smiling* (Capitol 11164)

1974 *Ice Water* (Capitol 11262)

1974 *Dreams And All That Stuff* (Capitol 11335)

1974 *Kottke/Lang/Fahey* (Takoma 1040)

1975 *Chewing Pine* (Capitol 11446)

1976 *Leo Kottke: 1971-1976* (Capitol 11576)

1976 *Leo Kottke* (Chrysalis 1106)

1978 *Leo Kottke: The Best* (Capitol SWBC-11867)

1978 *Burnt Lips* (Chrysalis 1191)

1979 *Balance* (Chrysalis 1234)

1980 *Live In Europe* (Chrysalis 1284)

1981 *Guitar Music* (Chrysalis 1328)

1983 *Time Step* (Chrysalis 41411)

1986 *A Shout Toward Noon* (Private Music 2007)

1988 *Regards From Chuck Pink* (Private Music 2025)

1989 *My Father's Face* (Private Music 2050)

1989 *Home & Away* (Private Music Video 2050-3-P)

1990 *That's What* (Private Music 2068)

1990 *Paul Bunyan* (Windham Hill 717)

1991 *Great Big Boy* (Private Music 82087)

1994 *Peculiaroso* (Private Music 82111)

Tablature Guide

Tablature (TAB) is a music notation system designed to show guitarists at which fret to depress a string when picking it. It has been in existence for centuries: Lutenists in the time of the European Renaissance used a distinctive form of tablature.

Tablature has two main advantages over standard notation: 1) it clearly indicates the position on the guitar neck of each note; and 2) it is much easier to learn to read. If you don't currently read either standard notation or tablature, I recommend that you learn to read tablature. You'll be playing the pieces in this book much sooner than if you take the time to learn standard notation.

Six horizontal lines represent the six strings of the guitar:

Ex. 1)

Notice in tablature that the bass string of the guitar is represented by the *bottom* line of the staff. The treble string is the *top* line. This is inverted from the way the strings actually lie on the guitar. The reason for the inversion is simply to make tablature look more like standard notation: the low-pitched notes are on the bottom lines of the staff, and the high-pitched notes are on the top lines.

A number on a line indicates at which fret to depress that string as you pick it. **Bold-type** numbers designate notes picked by the thumb. Lighter-type numbers are notes picked by the fingers, or are slurred notes (hammer-ons, pull-offs or slides):

Ex. 2)

In Example 2 you pick the strings in this order:

      1) fourth string open ("0" means an open string);
      2) the third string fretted at the 7th fret;
      3) the second string fretted at the 7th fret;
      4) the first (treble) string fretted at the 5th fret;
      5) then repeat the four notes.

The stems and beams underneath the notes denote the rhythm:

Ex. 3)

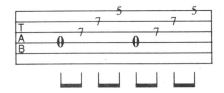

In Example 3, there are eight eighth-notes, each receiving one-half beat in 4/4 time. To produce the correct rhythm in Example 3, count evenly "1 & 2 & 3 & 4 &" along with the notes as you pick them.

Other rhythmic markings that you will see below the staff in this book are (in 4/4 time):

| = quarter note (1 beat) |⌐ = eighth note (1/2 beat)

|˙ = dotted quarter (1-1/2 beats)   ▬ = two sixteenth notes (1/2 beat)

ρ = half note (2 beats)   ▬▬ = four sixteenth notes (1 beat)

o = whole note (4 beats)   ⸼ = quarter-note rest (rest for 1 beat)

There are several other markings in the tablature that you will need to know as well.

◆12◆ = harmonic at the 12th fret   ─x─ = left- or right-hand damp (mute)

V · · · · = barre at the 5th fret   1/2 VII = barre over three strings, 7th fret

|⌒| = tie (sustain the note for the duration
         of the "tied" rhythmic markings)

"H" designates a hammer-on--sounding a note by fretting a string sharply with a finger of the left hand. "P" stands for pull-off--sounding a note by plucking a string with a finger of the left hand. "B" stands for bend--stretching the string to the side as the note is ringing.

"S" stands for slide--sounding a note by sliding to it from another fret position on that string. An ascending diagonal line (/) means to slide from a lower pitch to a higher pitch. A descending diagonal line means the opposite.

If a diagonal line directly connects two numbers, you sound the first note distinctly before sliding to the second. If a number is preceded by a diagonal line that is *not* connected to another number, then the left-hand finger must already be sliding on the string when you pick it. This technique provides the sound of the slide, but no distinct pitch before the notated number. For a number that is followed by a diagonal line *not* connected to another number, lift your finger off the string during the slide, before coming to rest on any particular fret.

A dot placed over a note or a chord designates "staccato." That means to release the note or chord immediately after it is picked. Most often this technique is accomplished by relaxing the fingers of the left hand, but not removing them from the strings. The fingers mute the strings, preventing what might otherwise sound like a pull-off.

A curly line next to a chord in the tablature means to strum the chord, or to arpeggiate the chord quickly with the fingers or thumb and fingers of the right hand.

For all of its attributes, tablature certainly has its disadvantages as well. The biggest deficiency of tablature is that it does not indicate how long to sustain each note. There are methods of indicating sustain in tablature, but they are difficult to read. The best solution to this problem is your sense of hearing. Listen closely to the instructional tape and to Kottke's original recordings to determine the duration of the notes. Then compare what you play to Leo's version.

Further Reading

Kottke In Print

Leo Kottke has had numerous magazine articles written about him during the course of his long solo career. Several of them have included transcriptions of his music. If you have been bitten by the Leo "bug" either through these transcriptions or from a different source, I highly recommend that you find these publications for more information on one of the true geniuses of fingerstyle guitar.

My first interview with Kottke was published in the May 1987 issue of *Frets Magazine*. Unfortunately, *Frets* no longer exists. It was discontinued in the summer of 1989. The 1987 interview included the standard notation and tablature for his classic instrumental "Fisherman," from *6- And 12-String Guitar*. Unfortunately, back issues of *Frets Magazine* are no longer available. But try your local music store or library if you are interested in finding a copy.

My second interview with Kottke was published in the January 1991 issue of *Guitar Player*. In addition to the main interview and an annotated version of "Little Beaver' (the entire version, first note to last, is printed in this book), lengthy discussions of his technique and equipment are included. My third Kottke interview was published in *Guitar Player's* April, '92 *Acoustic Revolution* issue. Another Kottke interview is available in *Guitar Player's* November, '87 issue. Back issues can be procured by writing to:

> *Guitar Player* Back Issues
> P.O. Box 2156,
> Knoxville, IA 50197-2156

A 1992 interview with Leo was published in *Acoustic Guitar Magazine*, Nov.-Dec. '92 issue. For a back issue, write them at

> *Acoustic Guitar Magazine*
> P.O. Box 767
> San Anselmo, CA 94979

A 1991 Kottke interview with a transcription of "Mona Ray" was published in *Guitar Extra Magazine*, Winter '91 issue. Write them at

> *Guitar Extra Magazine*
> 10 Midland Ave.
> Port Chester, NY 10573

Accent On Music makes available a number mid- to late-1980s Kottke tunes such as "William Powell," Times Twelve" and "A Trout Toward Noon." Two other books that include Kottke transcriptions are: *Leo Kottke--Eight Songs* and *20th Century Masters Of Fingerstyle Guitar*. They are available at your local music retailer.

Try to find as many of these publications as you can. You will have some fun with them!

Acknowledgements

My biggest thank you goes to Leo Kottke and Bug Music. Without their kind cooperation, fingerstyle guitarists everywhere would still be struggling to learn these tunes from Leo's recordings. Nearly as large a thank you goes to my wife Greta, daughters Marta and Johanna, and my parents for their substantial assistance in this project.

Others whose help and support was invaluable include DRUM! Magazine publisher Phil Hood, computer guru Patrick Mahoney at the MAC Resource Center, Jim Ferguson and Tom Wheeler of *Guitar Player Magazine,* recording magnate Charles Albert of Music Annex, Chris Ledgerwood for the cover design, Peter Fox for the cover photo, Pearwood Graphics, Dave McCumiskey of Music Sales, the crew at Gryphon Stringed Instruments in Palo Alto, and Kottke aficionado Tom Bowman, who keeps bugging me to do more of this stuff.

And, as always, I must thank the innumerable guitar students I have had over the past two decades. Your assistance in teaching me to teach is greatly appreciated.

About The Author

Mark Hanson worked as an Associate Editor and columnist at *Frets Magazine* until its demise in 1989. He is a performing guitarist as well as a writer, guitar instructor and publisher. He owns and operates Accent On Music, which publishes the *Acoustic Musician*™ Tape+TAB Series of taped guitar lessons, as well as his teaching methods on the alternating-bass style of fingerpicking guitar.

His interview subjects include such luminaries as James Taylor, David Crosby, Jorma Kaukonen and Larry Carlton. Mark also has interviewed Leo Kottke for both *Guitar Player* and *Frets.* Mark's accurate and thorough guitar transcriptions have appeared regularly in both publications.

Mark's background includes a music degree from Stanford University, and over twenty years of teaching and performing experience. Since the release of his album *Waterwheel* in 1976, Mark has continued to work as a recording guitarist, performer, and a promoter of acoustic guitar music of all styles.

Notes

Notes

Notation And Tablature Sheet

Notation And Tablature Sheet

Notation And Tablature Sheet

Notation And Tablature Sheet

Notation And Tablature Sheet

Notation And Tablature Sheet

Other Books By Mark Hanson And Accent On Music

Leo Kottke Transcribed

More high-quality Leo Kottke transcriptions, accompanied by Mark's measure-by-measure teaching cassette. Tunes include "William Powell," "Times Twelve," "A Trout Toward Noon" and "First To Go." Standard notation/TAB. Same format as *The Music Of Leo Kottke*.

Paul Simon Transcribed

Ten exact, note-for-note transcriptions from this great artist. Includes "Scarborough Fair," "Feelin' Groovy," "For Emily," "Kathy's Song," "Hearts and Bones," "Peace Like A River," and more. Standard notation/TAB, and thorough instruction for each tune.

The Art Of Contemporary Travis Picking

A comprehensive study of the patterns and variations of the modern alternating-bass fingerpicking guitar style. This book and 90-minute cassette take you from the basic patterns up through your first two solo pieces. All exercises and tunes are played at half- and full speed on the tape. Great for beginning fingerpickers and for more advanced players who want to understand this style. 14 tunes.

The Art Of Solo Fingerpicking
Recommended by Leo Kottke and John Renbourn.

This book and 90-minute cassette thoroughly describe the intermediate-to-advanced picking techniques associated with some of today's greatest fingerpicking masters. There are 13 solo instrumentals, plus "White House Blues" from John Renbourn. All exercises and tunes are played at half- and full speed on the tape. You'll add some hot techniques to your repertoire with this package. *Formerly Solo Style.*

The Acoustic Guitar Of Martin Simpson

This 80-page book contains exact, note-for-note transcriptions of 14 of this fingerstyle wizard's finest guitar instrumentals. Contents include lilting Celtic ballads, outrageous slide pyrotechnics, and Martin's explanation of his style and use of alternate tunings.

The Music of Mark Hanson---Standard & Drop-D Tunings

This booklet and 90-minute performance-and-teaching cassette tape feature four of Mark's original fingerstyle guitar compositions. The styles range from the Irish jig "Ryan Time (Again)," to the light-hearted pseudo-Bossa of "Parasol Spin." Also includes the guitar duet "Sweet Rotunda." Tablature only. TAB only. Contact Accent On Music for further details.

Beginning Slide Guitar

This book tells you all you need to know about slide technique: how to set up your guitar, types of slides and hand positions, damping, fretboard "visualization," playing slide in standard and open tunings, and much more. Includes appendixes on making your own bottleneck, recommended listening , and sources for slide guitar music. *Audio Teaching Cassette available through Accent On Music*

Alternate Tunings Guide For Guitar

Alternate guitar tunings are found almost everywhere in today's music. Form the recordings of balladeer Dan Fogelberg to those of heavy metal icon Jimmy Page, you'll find guitarists using alternate tunings. This book gives guitarists an understand of eight of the most commonly used guitar tunings. Includes a comprehensive list of well-known alternate-tuning pieces and their exact tunings.

Acoustic Jam Trax

Jam along with Mark and his band, the B-Street Irregulars, on 10 tunes covering a wide range of acoustic styles. Included are fingerstyle blues, swing, country, bluegrass, folk, a fiddle tune, a pop ballad, and-- just for fun--a James Brown-style acoustic funk groove. The accompanying book thoroughly describes how to solo over the band for each tune. Standard notation and tablature.

Acoustic Rock Jam Trax

More jam-along tunes from Mark and the B-Street Irregulars. This time we provide a rocking accompaniment to 10 rock tunes in the acoustic styles of Eric Clapton, Led Zeppelin, Extreme, Neil Young, the Black Crowes and more. As in *Acoustic Jam Trax*, the accompanying book thoroughly describes each tune and how to solo over the band. Standard notation and tablature.

12-String Guitar Guide

A great book for any guitarist interested in entering the exciting world of 12-string guitar. Guides you step-by-step through buying, stringing, and tuning your 12-string (standard and alternate tunings), and includes valuable tips on special playing techniques. Appendixes include recommended listening and reading, as well as a list of 12-string manufacturers and sources of 12-string recordings.

Distributed by Music Sales Inc., New York, NY
For more information, inquire at your local music dealer or contact
Accent On Music, 19363 Willamette Dr., #252
West Linn, OR 97068 USA (Address effective April, 1994)
(503) 699-1814

ORDER FORM

• ACOUSTIC MUSICIAN™ TAPE+TAB SERIES	Catalog Number	Price
The Music of Leo Kottke (book & cassette)	T 301	$19.95
Leo Kottke Transcribed (book & cassette)	T 302	$19.95
Mark Hanson: Standard & Drop-D Tunings (book & cassette)	T 201	$17.95

INSTRUCTION BOOKS	Catalog Number	Price
Paul Simon Transcribed (book)	AM 4044	$19.95
The Acoustic Guitar of Martin Simpson (book)	AM 5044	$17.95
Contemporary Travis Fingerpicking Series:		
Art of Contemporary Travis Picking (book & cassette)	AM 1044	$18.95
Art of Solo Fingerpicking (formerly *Solo Style*) (book & cassette)	AM 2044	$18.95

Guitar Case Series		
Acoustic Jam Trax (All styles: Blues, Folk, Country, Rock, Funk)	MS 040	$12.95
Acoustic Rock Jam Trax (Acoustic Rock)	MS 050	$12.95
The Alternate Tunings Guide for Guitar	MS 010	$ 5.95
Beginning Slide Guitar (book & cassette)	MS 020	$12.95
12-String Guitar Guide	MS 030	$ 5.95

Catalog No.	Product	Quantity x	Unit Price =	Amount

SUBTOTAL $_____

SHIPPING AND HANDLING

U.S. orders: Add $4.50 for first unit, $1.50 for each additional unit

Canadian orders: Add $5.00 for first unit, $1.50 for each additional unit $_____

Add $2.00 for Priority Mail $_____

OVERSEAS AIRMAIL:

For Tape+TAB and Instruction Books: Add $10.50 for first unit, $3.50 for each additional.

For Guitar Case Series: Add $7.00 for first unit, $2.00 for each additional. $_____

TOTAL: $_____

TO ORDER:

Call (503) 699-1814, or send VISA/MASTERCARD/CHECK/MONEY ORDER (US$ drawn on a US bank), payable to:
Accent On Music, 19363 Willamette Dr. #252, West Linn, OR 97068 USA (Address effective April, 1994)
Refund (excluding shipping) within 30 days only.

Name _____

Address _____

City, State, ZIP _____

Country _____ Telephone No. (_____)_____

VISA/MC No. __ __ __ __ - __ __ __ __ - __ __ __ __ - __ __ __ __   Exp. Date__ __-__ __

Signature _____